Allison Lassieur

Scorpions

The Sneaky Stingers

Franklin Watts - A Division of Grolier Publishing
New York • London • Hong Kong • Sydney • Danbury, Connecticut

Photographs ©: Animals Animals: 1, 39 (LSF/OSF); Brian Kenney: 25; Dr. Scott A. Stockwell: 40; Michael Cardwell & Associates: 12, 13, 15, 30, 31, 33; NHPA: 37 (Daniel Heuclin), 35 (Haroldo Palo, Jr.); Peter Arnold Inc.: 5 bottom right (John Cancalosi), 20, 21 (James Gerholdt), 29 (IFA), 27 (Matt Meadows); Photo Researchers: 7 (David T. Roberts); Place Stock Photo: 43 (Bruce Farnsworth); Robert & Linda Mitchell: cover, 6, 17, 19, 23, 41; Visuals Unlimited: 5 top right (Bill Beatty), 5 bottom left (R. Calentine), 5 top left (G. & C. Merker).

Illustrations by Jose Gonzales and Steve Savage

The photo on the cover shows a swollen-stinger scorpion. The photo on the title page shows two Israeli gold scorpions fighting.

┌───┐
│ Visit Franklin Watts on the Internet at: │
│   http://publishing.grolier.com   │
└───┘

Library of Congress Cataloging-in-Publication Data

Lassieur, Allison.
    Scorpions, the sneaky stingers / Allison Lassieur.
        p. cm. — (Animals in order)
    Includes bibliographical references and index.
    Summary: Discusses the order of the animal kingdom known as scorpions and describes the members of fifteen different species that are found in the Americas, Africa, Europe, and Israel.
    ISBN 0-531-11651-4   (lib. bdg.)   0-531-16497-7 (pbk.)
    Scorpions—juvenile literature. [Scorpions.] I. Title. II. Series.
QL458.7.L27   2000
595.4'6—dc211   99-42709

GROLIER
PUBLISHING   2 3 4 5 6 7 8 9 10 R 09 08 07 06 05 04 03

Contents

Scorpion Alert!

Sneaky, scary, deadly—those are just a few words people use to describe scorpions. These fierce-looking little creatures have a reputation from way back. The ancient Egyptians wrote about how to get rid of scorpions. People who lived in ancient Babylonia, one of the world's first civilizations, feared and respected scorpions so much that they named a star group, Scorpio, after them. Even today, people steer clear of the crawling, stinging critters whenever they can.

Some scorpions can make people sick. A few have such strong *venom* or enough venom in their stingers to kill, but most scorpions do not harm people.

Scorpions are not insects. They are more closely related to spiders, ticks, and mites. Look at the four pictures on the next page. Can you figure out why scientists have placed scorpions in the same group as spiders, ticks, and mites?

Stripe-tail devil scorpion

Wood tick

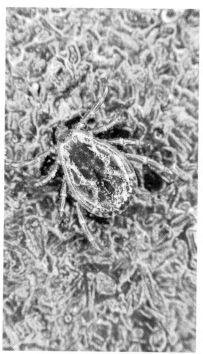

Red spider mite

Tarantula

Traits of a Scorpion

Did you count the legs of these animals? They all have eight legs. Insects belong to a different group because they have only six legs. A scorpion's front pair of "legs" don't look like most legs. Over time, they have developed into special structures called *pedipalps*. Spiders have pedipalps too. Spiders and scorpions use their pedipalps to grab and hold *prey* and to defend themselves against enemies.

A scorpion's body has two parts. The front part is made up of the head and chest. The back part looks like a long, curling tail—but it isn't really a tail at all. At the end of this section, the scorpion packs a nasty surprise—its stinger. A scorpion uses its stinger to inject poi-

This is what a scorpion's stinger looks like up close.

sonous venom into its prey. Most scorpions eat insects and other small creatures. Some larger scorpions eat lizards and mice—and even other scorpions.

A scorpion is the only animal that has a pair of body parts called *pectines*. Pectines are comblike structures with teeth along the edges. They are used to sense vibrations, or movements. Scorpions are active at night, so scientists think that pectines may help scorpions find their way in the darkness.

Many scorpions live in deserts. Others like trees and plants. A few species live deep inside caves. One kind of scorpion lives high in the Himalaya mountains. Scorpions live in every part of the world except Antarctica, but most are found in the United States, Mexico, and Africa.

is scorpion is attacking a cricket.

The Order of Living Things

A tiger has more in common with a house cat than with a daisy. A true bug is more like a butterfly than a jellyfish. Scientists arrange living things into groups based on how they look and how they act. A tiger and a house cat belong to the same group, but a daisy belongs to a different group.

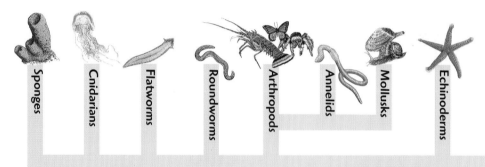

Sponges | Cnidarians | Flatworms | Roundworms | Arthropods | Annelids | Mollusks | Echinoderms

Animals

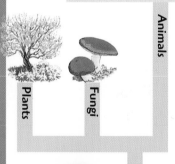

Plants | Fungi

Monerans | Protists

All living things can be placed in one of five groups called *kingdoms*: the plant kingdom, the animal kingdom, the fungus kingdom, the moneran kingdom, or the protist kingdom. You can probably name many of the creatures in the plant and animal kingdoms. The fungus kingdom includes mushrooms, yeasts, and molds. The moneran and protist kingdoms contain thousands of living things that are too small to see without a microscope.

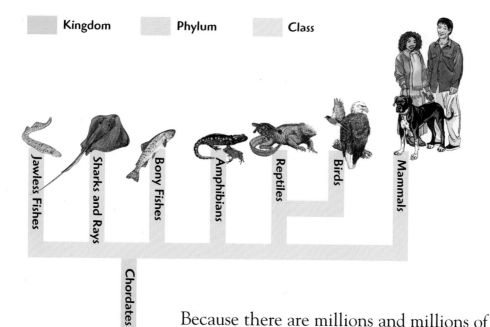

Kingdom Phylum Class

Jawless Fishes

Sharks and Rays

Bony Fishes

Amphibians

Reptiles

Birds

Mammals

Chordates

Because there are millions and millions of living things on Earth, some of the members of one kingdom may not seem all that similar. The animal kingdom includes creatures as different as tarantulas and trout, jellyfish and jaguars, salamanders and sparrows, elephants and earthworms.

To show that an elephant is more like a jaguar than an earthworm, scientists further separate the creatures in each kingdom into more specific groups. The animal kingdom can be divided into nine *phyla*. Humans belong to the chordate phylum. Almost all chordates have a backbone.

Each phylum can be subdivided into many *classes*. Humans, mice, and elephants all belong to the mammal class. Each class can be further divided into *orders*; orders into *families*, families into *genera*, and genera into *species*. All the members of a species are very similar.

How Scorpions Fit In

You can probably guess that scorpions belong to the animal kingdom. They have more in common with snakes and spiders than with maple trees and morning glories.

Scorpions belong to the arthropod phylum. This is the largest group in the animal kingdom. Arthropods are invertebrates, which means they do not have a skeleton. They do have a tough outer skin called an *exoskeleton* that protects the soft tissues that make up their bodies. Can you guess what other living things might be arthropods? Examples include insects, spiders, mites, ticks, millipedes, and centipedes. Other arthropods live in the ocean. Lobsters, crabs, and shrimps are all arthropods.

The arthropod phylum can be divided into a number of classes. Scorpions belong to the arachnid class. Spiders, ticks, and mites are also arachnids.

There are eleven orders of arachnids. Scorpions make up one of these orders. Scorpions have more eyes than other arachnids. Some species have as many as six pairs.

Scorpions can be divided into a number of families and genera. At least 1,500 kinds of scorpions live in the world. Some scientists think that there may be hundreds more that haven't been discovered yet.

This book will introduce you to fifteen species of scorpions. Even though they have a nasty reputation, most scorpions aren't dangerous.

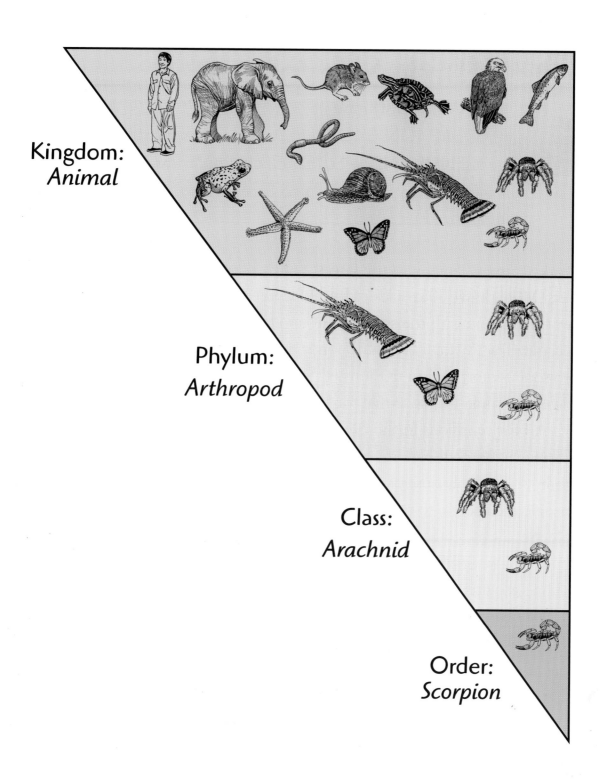

Kingdom: *Animal*

Phylum: *Arthropod*

Class: *Arachnid*

Order: *Scorpion*

Bark Scorpions

FAMILY: Buthidae
COMMON EXAMPLE: Arizona bark scorpion
GENUS AND SPECIES: *Centruroides exilicauda*
SIZE: 2 to 3 inches (5 to 8 cm)

Bark scorpions belong to the largest family of scorpions. More than 300 species of Buthidae live in the world, including all the species that are dangerous to people. The Arizona bark scorpion is one of the most poisonous scorpions in the United States, but it isn't as deadly as some people think.

All the scorpions in the Buthidae family have strong venom, but bark scorpions are usually too small to inject a deadly dose of venom into a person. Some people are allergic to scorpion stings, just as some people are allergic to bee stings. If these people are stung by a bark scorpion, they may die. Small children and old people are most sensitive to a bark scorpion's sting.

The bark scorpion lives under the bark of trees. That's where it gets its name. It's not picky about hiding places though. In a pinch, a bark scorpion will crawl under a rock, a log, or even inside a sneaker.

This tree-dwelling scorpion will either hunt for prey or just sit still and hope that dinner will stroll by. If a

12

small insect or other prey comes close enough, the bark scorpion grabs the prey with its pedipalps and holds on.

The bark scorpion can stretch the tail-like part of its body over its head to sting prey that is in front of it. That's a good trick! The last thing an unlucky insect sees is that deadly stinger.

Giant Scorpions

FAMILY: Iuridae
COMMON EXAMPLE: Giant hairy scorpion
GENUS AND SPECIES: *Hadrurus arizonensis*
SIZE: 4 to 7 inches (10 to 18 cm)

This gigantic arachnid is hard to miss. The giant hairy scorpion is the largest scorpion found in North America. It lives in the deserts of California and Arizona and in some parts of Mexico.

Scorpions that live in desert areas don't usually drink water, but scientists have seen a few scorpions drink from puddles after a rainstorm. Giant hairy scorpions get all the water they need from their environment and from the animals they eat. That's why they're often found in places where a lot of building is going on. Wet concrete and piles of damp lumber provide the kind of wet, humid homes they like.

Giant hairy scorpions also hide under objects scattered across the desert floor and sometimes burrow in the sand, especially if the sand is loose. In summer, when the desert gets very hot, they hide wherever they can. They make their homes under rocks or logs or even in people's sleeping bags.

Have you ever noticed all the "hairs" on a scorpion's legs? Those structures aren't really hair. They are sensors that help the scorpion catch prey. Whenever prey crawls by, the sensors can feel the air move. If the prey gets close enough, the scorpion's pincers snap up the little animal. After injecting a deadly dose of venom, it's lunchtime!

Sand Scorpions

FAMILY: Vaejovidae
COMMON EXAMPLE: Giant sand scorpion
GENUS AND SPECIES: *Smeringurus mesaensis*
SIZE: 3 inches (8 cm)

Giant sand scorpions live in the deserts of Arizona and southeastern California, but even if you visit these areas you probably won't see one. Most have a yellowish exoskeleton that blends in with their sandy surroundings.

Like all scorpions, the giant sand scorpion *molts*, or sheds its exoskeleton, as it grows. Whenever a scorpion's old skin gets too small, it splits open and the scorpion climbs out with the new, larger exoskeleton in place. At first the new covering is soft and flexible, but after a few days it hardens. A giant hairy scorpion often molts seven or eight times before it is fully grown.

Most scorpions eat insects, moths, and small animals such as lizards or mice. That's not true of the giant sand scorpion though. Its favorite food is other giant sand scorpions! If it can't have a relative for dinner, it will make do with other kinds of scorpions.

Like many sand scorpions, the giant sand scorpion has very poor eyesight. To find prey, it depends on its ability to feel vibrations in the sand. If another scorpion starts digging a burrow, a giant sand scorpion can feel it. The hungry *predator* finds just the right spot and digs out its prey. The giant sand scorpion kills the other animal and has a crunchy scorpion feast.

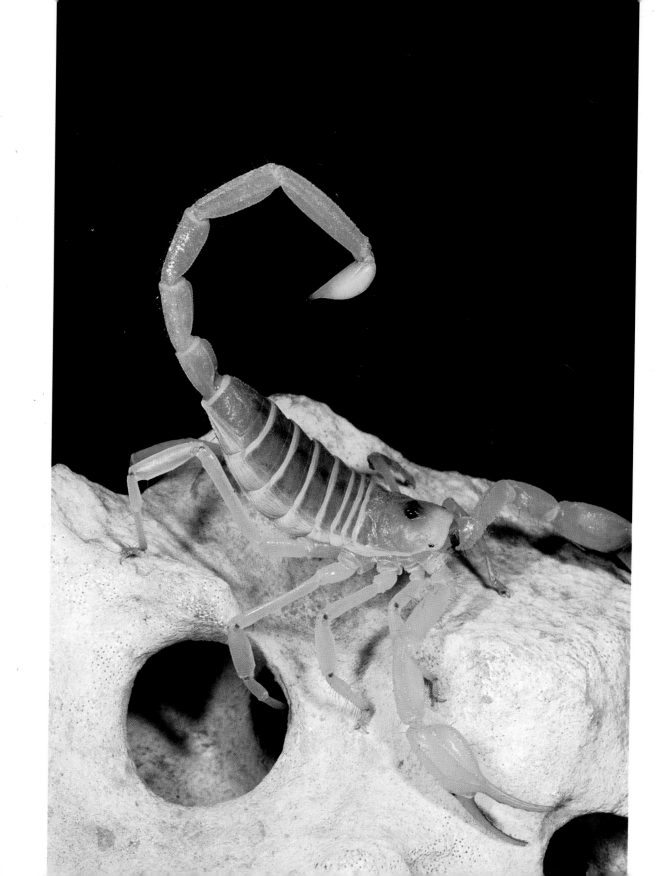

Striped Scorpions

FAMILY: Buthidae
COMMON EXAMPLE: Striped scorpion
GENUS AND SPECIES: *Centruroides vittatus*
SIZE: 2 1/2 inches (6 cm)

Can you see the stripes on the back of this scorpion? Older striped scorpions are dark with light stripes. Younger scorpions look clear and have darker stripes. This scorpion gets part of its name, *vittatus*, from the Latin word for "striped."

If you ever see a scorpion where you live, chances are it is a striped scorpion. People in the United States see this species of scorpion more often than any other. That's because they often find these scorpions living inside people's homes. The striped scorpion has been spotted from New Mexico to Florida, as far north as Oklahoma, and south into Texas and Mexico.

Part of the reason that striped scorpions get so much attention is because they can live almost anywhere. They like closed-in places, such as narrow cracks between rocks. They also live in grasslands and sand dunes. That's why they are sometimes called plains scorpions or wood scorpions. Most scorpions live alone, but some striped scorpions live in groups called colonies.

The striped scorpion is venomous and can deliver a painful sting. Scientists don't know why, but people say this scorpion's sting hurts most in March or April.

19

Desert Scorpions

FAMILY: Vaejovidae
COMMON EXAMPLE: Stripe-tail devil scorpion
GENUS AND SPECIES: *Vaejovis spinigerus*
SIZE: 2 inches (5 cm)

This scorpions's name makes it sound very dangerous, but it isn't nearly as ferocious as you might think. It is venomous, but its poison is not very strong.

The stripe-tail devil scorpion lives in many areas of the southwestern United States and has been seen as far north as Illinois. It likes to hide under dead cactuses, wood scraps, and rocks. Sleeping bags and shoes also make good hideouts for this scorpion. When the scorpion finds a good spot, it digs a short burrow, or "scrape." In the Sonoran desert in Mexico, however, the stripe-tail devil scorpion digs burrows up to 3 feet (1 m) deep.

All scorpions, including the stripe-tail devil scorpion, stake out *territories* for hunting. Sometimes a scorpion will stay in the same spot for days, waiting for prey to crawl by. If nothing appears, the scorpion will move to a better spot.

Stripe-tail devil scorpions are usually found near dry desert riverbeds or in places carved out by running water. Sometimes people build homes in the places scorpions like to live. When the summer rains come, watch out! In desert areas, heavy rains can cause sudden floods. Scorpions caught in floodwaters may move into houses until the water goes down.

Burrowing Scorpions

FAMILY: Iuridae

COMMON EXAMPLE: Swollen-stinger scorpion

GENUS AND SPECIES: *Anuroctonus*
  phaiodactylus

SIZE: 2 to 3 inches (5 to 8 cm)

Look at the end of this scorpion's tail where the stinger is. Can you see how this scorpion got its name? It's also called the dusky-footed scorpion. Check out the dark color at the ends of those huge pincers. It's easy to see where that name came from too.

Swollen-stinger scorpions can be found from southern California all the way up to Idaho. They build their homes in packed, sandy ground in hilly areas where trees and bushes grow. They don't seem to like loose sand or bare ground.

Swollen-stinger scorpions love to make burrows, just as many other scorpions do. These scorpions rarely come out though! They spend almost their whole lives underground. Males come out only to find a mate. Females stay in their own burrows, waiting for males to find them.

If the scorpions never come out, how do they find food? They don't. They just wait for a confused insect or another small creature to fall into their burrow. When that happens, the scorpion grabs it with those huge pincers. There isn't any room in the burrow for the scorpion to use its stinger, so it crushes its prey instead.

Venomous Scorpions

FAMILY: Buthidae

COMMON EXAMPLE: Black square-tailed scorpion

GENUS AND SPECIES: *Parabuthus transvaalicus*

SIZE: 2 to 5 inches (5 to 13 cm)

Warning: This scorpion can surprise you. The black square-tailed scorpion belongs to the Buthidae family. That means it's venomous. Its venom isn't that strong though. So why the warning?

This scorpion has an unusual, and often surprising, way of using its venom. It can squirt venom, as a cobra does, more than 24 inches (61 cm). If the venom gets into a person's eyes, it hurts a lot—and it can do serious damage. It may even cause blindness.

Using its large "tail" as a squirt gun also means that this scorpion can blast more venom at its victim. The heavy dose is sometimes enough to kill. The good news is that there is an *antidote* that will prevent or lessen the effects of this venom. Few people die because of venom squirts from this scorpion.

Like other scorpions, the black square-tailed scorpion does not go out of its way to attack animals it doesn't recognize as food. This scorpion was named *transvaalicus* because it lives in a region in South Africa called the Transvaal. This area is rich in diamonds and gold. The first European miners to dig for minerals were probably very surprised when they met their fellow burrowers.

Pet Scorpions

FAMILY: Scorpionidae
COMMON EXAMPLE: Emperor scorpion
GENUS AND SPECIES: *Pandinus imperator*
SIZE: 5 to 9 inches (9 to 23 cm)

People who keep scorpions as pets usually have emperor scorpions. It's one of the easiest scorpions to raise in captivity. The emperor scorpion will eat just about any animal smaller than itself. Lizards and mice make yummy meals—so do other scorpions.

Emperor scorpions look impressive. They are usually shiny black and grow fairly large. They don't fight much though, and they don't sting too often. That's why people like them.

You can tell how venomous a scorpion is by looking at its pedipalps. The bigger the pedipalps are, the less venomous the scorpion is. The emperor scorpion has huge pincers. How poisonous do you think it is? Emperor scorpions usually don't use their stingers to kill their food. They use their pedipalps instead.

Like other scorpions, when a female emperor scorpion has young, she carries them around on her back. She may sound like a nice mom, but babies beware! It's not unusual for a female scorpion to eat her young.

Young scorpions leave their mothers' backs after their first molt, usually a couple of weeks after they are born. If the young return to the mother's burrow for some reason, they can easily become prey.

Coastal Scorpions

FAMILY: Buthidae

COMMON EXAMPLE: Mediterranean yellow scorpion

GENUS AND SPECIES: *Buthus occitanus*

SIZE: 2 to 3 inches (5 to 8 cm)

If you turn over a rock on a dry, stony beach on the Mediterranean coast, you might find one of these golden scorpions. Then, if you're smart, you'll walk away—fast.

This scorpion has long, thin pedipalps. The size of those pincers tells you that the animal is probably poisonous. The smaller the pincers, the more deadly the scorpion can be. Mediterranean yellow scorpions don't usually kill people though.

The Mediterranean yellow scorpion lives in coastal areas. They are often found under rocks that are near water. Millions of years ago, all scorpions lived in the water. Scientists have found *fossils* of these ancient scorpions. A fossil is the remains of a dead animal that has been preserved in Earth's crust. A fossil can also be an outline or an impression of anything that was once alive.

The fossils of ancient scorpions look almost exactly like scorpions living today. That makes the scorpion one of the world's oldest animals. Some people call scorpions "living fossils" because they have changed very little over millions of years.

Rock Scorpions

FAMILY: Ischnuridae

COMMON EXAMPLE: South African rock scorpion

GENUS AND SPECIES: *Hadogenes troglodytes*

SIZE: 8 to 9 inches (20 to 23 cm)

The South African rock scorpion has a big claim to fame. It's the longest scorpion species in the world. Some people have reported seeing rock scorpions that are 12 inches (30 cm) long, but most members of this species are a little smaller than that.

Take a ruler and measure your hand from the wrist to the tip of your middle finger. Would you be able to hold a rock scorpion in one hand?

Even if you could hold one, it's not likely that you'd ever get close enough to try. Rock scorpions live in the cracks of large stones in the mountains of South Africa. Notice how flat the scorpion's body is? That helps it squeeze inside tiny spaces between rocks.

The rock scorpion uses its giant pedipalps for two things. They are great for gripping rocks so this scorpion is a good climber. The scorpion also uses its pincers to kill prey. Those huge claws are powerful enough to draw blood from any person who tries to pick it up.

31

Dangerous Scorpions

FAMILY: Buthidae

COMMON EXAMPLE: Yellow fat-tail scorpion

GENUS AND SPECIES: *Androctonus australis*

SIZE: 3 to 4 inches (8 to 10 cm)

Big and dangerous—that's the yellow fat-tail scorpion. It's the most dangerous scorpion in the world. More people die from the sting of this scorpion than from any other. Its venom is very strong. Drop for drop, the yellow fat-tail scorpion's venom is as deadly as a cobra's. Its scientific name means "southern man-killer."

This scorpion is very common in North African countries, such as Tunisia and Egypt, and in some countries in the Middle East. The yellow fat-tail seems to favor the same kind of *habitats* as humans. People often find yellow fat-tail scorpions in their closets, under their furniture, and even in their shoes.

The yellow fat-tail scorpion doesn't mess around. It moves fast and stings quickly. Sometimes it stings so quickly that a person doesn't even realize what's happening—until it's too late. In Tunisia, more than 200 people die every year from the sting of a yellow fat-tail scorpion. Most victims are children, older people, or people in poor health.

That fat "tail" isn't just for stinging though. The yellow fat-tail also uses the back of its body like a mini-bulldozer to dig out burrows.

South American Scorpions

FAMILY: Buthidae

COMMON EXAMPLE: Brazilian yellow scorpion

GENUS AND SPECIES: *Tityus serrulatus*

SIZE: 2 to 3 inches (5 to 8 cm)

Termites and scorpions—you might not imagine that you'd find them in the same place. In the grasslands of South America, however, the best place to find Brazilian yellow scorpions is in termite nests. The Brazilian yellow scorpion is the most venomous scorpion in Brazil, and it is one of the most dangerous scorpions in the world.

Brazilian yellow scorpions wouldn't worry people if they stayed in the countryside, but they don't. If their termite homes are destroyed, these scorpions may move to the city. Sometimes they hitch rides on passing trucks or hide in food products that are shipped to areas where a lot of people live.

The strangest thing about the Brazilian yellow scorpion is that the species has no males. All the scorpions in this species are female. The females don't need males to *fertilize* their eggs. Their ability to reproduce without males is called *parthenogenesis*. When Brazilian yellow scorpion females do have young, all of them are females too.

Brazilian yellow scorpions treat their young like other scorpions do. The mothers carry their young around on their backs until they molt for the first time.

European Scorpions

FAMILY: Chactidae
COMMON NAME: European scorpion
GENUS AND SPECIES: *Euscorpius flavicaudis*
SIZE: 1 to 2 inches (2.5 to 5 cm)

Not many scorpions make their homes in Europe. As a matter of fact, the European scorpion is one of only a few kinds of scorpions that live in European countries around the Mediterranean Sea. It lives in the southern part of England, the south of France, and northern Italy. In England, this scorpion was first sighted at seaports. The first European scorpions to arrive in England were probably stowaways on ships sailing from ports in mainland Europe.

This small scorpion hides out in the cracks of rocks and between bricks. It's not easy to find, even in places where many of these scorpions live. They rarely sting people, but even when they do, there is little danger. This scorpion has very weak venom.

Another member of this scorpion family lives in the mountains of Italy and Switzerland. A third relative can be found along the shores and islands of the Mediterranean Sea. Still another likes the safety of cracks in the dry stone walls of Italian houses. A cave-living member of the family lives deep underneath the Pyrenees mountains in France. That scorpion is white and has no eyes.

Middle Eastern Scorpions

FAMILY: Scorpionidae
COMMON EXAMPLE: Israeli gold scorpion
GENUS AND SPECIES: *Scorpio maurus*
SIZE: 3 inches (7.5 cm)

This busy traveler can be found throughout the Middle East and even in Africa. The Israeli gold scorpion has been found in almost every kind of habitat. It lives in deserts, on grasslands, and on mountains and other rocky places. It can live in low-lying areas and on the tops of the Atlas mountains.

In the desert, Israeli gold scorpions burrow deep into the sandy soil. If they can't dig burrows, they don't live very long. No one knows why. This kind of burrower is called an obligate (ah-BLIH-guht) burrower. Obligate means the animal must, or is obligated to, dig a burrow.

Israeli gold scorpions live in colonies in which many members of the species dig burrows near one another. These burrows can be up to 27 inches (69 cm) deep. That depth helps protect the animals from the harsh desert climate.

The Israeli gold scorpion was the first scorpion that modern scientists named. At one time, the genus name *Scorpio* was the name used for all scorpions. Another name for this animal is the large-clawed yellow scorpion. Can you see why? Those powerful pincers can crush

prey with one snap. They are even strong enough to move rocks as
big as the scorpion's whole body.

What else do those huge pedipalps tell you? Israeli gold scorpions
aren't very likely to sting. They use their pedipalps, not their
stingers, to kill their prey and defend themselves.

The Life of a Scorpion Hunter

Turn over a rock. Underneath, a nasty-looking scorpion lurks. Most people would run away, but not Scott Stockwell. He's had plenty of experience with scorpions. When he comes across a scorpion, he usually reaches down and picks it up—with his bare hands.

Stockwell is an *entomologist* —a scientist who studies insects. He studies mosquitoes for the U.S. Army. But Stockwell's real love is scorpions. "They're interesting animals," he says. "There are so many different kinds of scorpions. They have been around more than 420 million years, almost unchanged."

Stockwell became interested in scorpions when he was in college, and he's studied them

Scott Stockwell holding a giant hairy scorpion

A giant hairy scorpion

ever since. He even has a website devoted to scorpions. It's called the Scorpion Emporium.

Stockwell's main goal is to discover new species of scorpions. When he is successful, he gets a bonus—he can name the new animal. "I'm the guy who comes up with all those names, those scientific names, that nobody wants to learn to say," he says. "I get to describe all the species."

Stockwell's search for new scorpions takes him all over the world. "Scorpions live in lots of different habitats. You find them everywhere," he says. When he's on a scorpion search, Stockwell arms himself with some low-tech gear: a rock roller, a black (ultraviolet) light, and some small plastic bags. He doesn't use gloves or any other protective gear. "I just pick up the scorpions and drop them in the bag."

After Stockwell locates a prime scorpion hunting ground, the search begins. "I look under rocks, logs, or any other type of surface object," he says. "Sometimes I even roll over dead animals to find scorpions. I just hold my breath and hope I'll find something worthwhile."

At night, Stockwell shines a black light along the ground, at trees, or anywhere he thinks a scorpion might be. "Because scorpions glow under black light, it's easy to find them in the dark," he says. When Stockwell sees a bright blue or green glow, he knows he's spotted a scorpion.

How many times has Stockwell been stung? "Oh, hundreds and hundreds," he says. "Scorpions get a bad rap because they're venemous. The truth is that most scorpions aren't very dangerous to humans.

"The problem is that people who get stung tend to freak out," Stockwell continues. "It's very painful and people think they're going to die. The best thing to do is stay calm."

Scientists aren't sure why scorpions glow when a black light shines on them.

Words to Know

antidote—a substance that prevents or counteracts the effects of poison

class—a group of creatures within a phylum that share certain characteristics

entomologist—a scientist who studies insects

exoskeleton—a tough, bonelike outer skin that protects an animal

family—a group of creatures within an order that share certain characteristics

fertilize—to mix eggs and sperm to create a new individual

fossil—the hardened remains of ancient plant or animal matter

genus (plural **genera**)—a group of creatures within a family that share certain characteristics

habitat—the environment where a plant or animal lives and grows

kingdom—one of the five divisions into which all living things are placed: the animal kingdom, the plant kingdom, the fungus kingdom, the moneran kingdom, and the protist kingdom

molt—to shed an exoskeleton

order—a group of organisms within a class that share certain characteristics

parthenogenesis—reproduction without males

pectine—a sensory structure on the underside of a scorpion's body

pedipalp—a leglike structure ending in a clawlike structure that an arachnid uses for capturing prey and defending itself

phylum (plural **phyla**)—a group of animals within a kingdom that share certain characteristics

predator—an animal that hunts other animals for food

prey—an animal hunted for food by another animal

species—a group of organisms within a genus that share certain characteristics. Members of a species can mate and produce young.

territory—the area where an animal hunts and raises its young

venom—a poison injected into prey or enemies

Learning More

Books

Cooper, Jason. *Scorpions*. New York: Vero Beach, FL: Rourke Publishing Group, 1996.

Hillyard, Paul. *Spiders and Scorpions*. Pleasantville, NY: Reader's Digest, 1995.

Pringle, Lawrence. *Scorpion Man: Exploring the World of Scorpions*. New York: Charles Scribner's Sons, 1994.

Web Sites

The Arachnology Home Page
http://www.ufsia.be/Arachnology/Arachnology.html
This huge site bills itself as the "arachnology hub of the World Wide Web." It is. The site lists dozens of web links, mailing lists, discussion groups, and photo sites about all arachnids, including scorpions.

Desert USA
http://www.Desertusa.com/in dex.html
This site has lots of information about desert life, including a section about scorpions and their venom.

Scorpion Emporium
http://wrbu.si.edu/WWW/Stockwell/emporium/emporium.html
This site has all kinds of photos and information about scorpions around the world.

Index

About the Author

Allison Lassieur loves writing about history, animals, and science—the grosser the better. She has written more than two dozen books about history, cultures, current events, animals, natural disasters, transportation, and Native Americans. She has also written *Head Lice*, which is all about those creepy crawly critters that can invade people's hair.

Ms. Lassieur has also written magazine articles for *National Geographic World*, *Scholastic News*, *Highlights for Children*, and *Disney Adventures*. When Ms. Lassieur isn't writing, she enjoys reading, hanging out with friends, and making medieval costumes.